LAYLA

A gift for

GRAMMA +

From

GRAMPA

Tiny Tidings of Joy

for You, Grandchild

Illustrations by Jeannie Mooney

COUNTRYMAN

Published by J. Countryman,
a division of Thomas Nelson, Inc.,
Nashville, Tennessee 37214

Project Editor: Terri Gibbs

Designed by Left Coast Design Inc., Portland, Oregon

ISBN: 08499-9672-4

www.jcountryman.com

Printed in Singapore

A tiny tiding
sent to say,
"Have a happy
Christmas day!"

Christmas treasures
here and there,
surprises scattered
everywhere.
But the treasure
I would choose,
is the treasure
that is you!

A song of love heard in the night,
a song from above when stars glow bright.

Let me tell you how I love you:

I love that your life is so new, bright + full of hope. I love how you look at your Mom + Dad — you already give love.

Glowing cheeks
and sparkling eyes,
packages just waiting
to surprise;
from the moment
Christmas starts
it brings joy into
our hearts.

Christmas dreams are brushed

with angel wings.

You won't find
the best gift
underneath the tree,
for it's the gift of
the love in my heart—
a gift for you . . .
from me!

Love
came
down at
Christmas,

Love
all lovely,
Love
divine.

-Christina Rosetti

God loves you

snow ♥ much!

And
I do
too!!!

A shining light
a twinkling star,
a chance to say
how special I
think you
are!

Some of the things that make you special:

You cute sparkley eyes
+ rosey cheeks.

Christmas is the time of year when loving hearts are gathered near.

Candy canes
of red and white,
Candles glowing
warm and bright,
Christmas time
is coming near,
Let's spread
around joy and
good cheer.

Every gift given in love . . .

is given well.

May your days
be filled with love
and laughter...
not only
at Christmas
but ever
after.

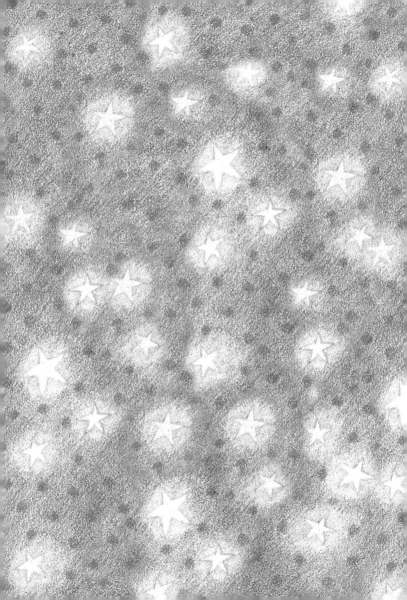